Table of Contents

About Music and Singing page 7

Animals and Critters page 25

Friendship, Love, Peace and Conflict page 37

Humorous and Clever page 55

Meals and Blessings page 75

Morning and Evening page 79

Nature, Land and Sea page 101

On Death and Dying page 113

People, Places and Things page 121

Sacred and Latin page 143

Seasons page 163

Songs without Words page 171

Introduction

Rounds and canons have been enjoyed since the Elizabethan era. And, although many are anonymous, it is not likely they could be called folk songs as few common "folk" created songs in counterpoint. Indeed, some of the great composers throughout history have created clever canons, some simple and some not so simple.

The premise of a canon is that it is a single song that can be sung starting at different times creating lovely harmonies. Most often the entrances are in the same key, although you will find some canons in this collection that have entrances in other keys/modes making for even more clever compositions.

Some of the examples in this collection are sung with each part entering after the other and then each part ending after the other. Other canons can be performed with cadence points when everyone stops at the same time ending on a harmonic chord. Those cadence points are marked with either a "down bow" mark (⊓) or a fermata (⌢). Note that these marks are only observed at the final cadence and ignored otherwise.

For your convenience difficulty levels have been indicated. Ideally, the easiest ones might be taught to students in the third grade or older. As the great children's choir director Helen Kemp used to say, "It is much more important to have children sing beautifully in unison than to sing badly in parts." Canons marked medium-difficult or difficult are

Revised Edition

THE BOOK OF
Canons

Compiled by John M. Feierabend

GIA PUBLICATIONS, INC. * CHICAGO

Compiled by
John M. Feierabend

G-8552
Copyright © 2014, 2022
GIA Publications, Inc.
7404 S. Mason Avenue
Chicago, IL 60638

Printed in the
United States of America.
ISBN: 978-1-62277-687-0

worthy of the pleasure and/or performance of high school or even college choirs.

In the elementary grades students should enjoy singing the song in unison for two or three lessons. Then, see if the class can sing the song while the teacher sings it in canon with the class. Later divide the class into two parts and only after they can succeed in two parts attempt the canon in its full version of three, four, or five parts.

It is best to repeat a canon enough times so that the last part to enter has had the opportunity to sing the entire song at least two times. That way the final part can enjoy the full harmonic interaction with the other parts.

For those examples in foreign languages, "general translations" have been provided so the singer can best understand the spirit of the song. These translations are not provided (or suitable) for singing. Songs should be sung in their original language.

Here then is a collection to meet many needs, sacred and secular, humorous and serious, major, minor and modal, simple to complex.... but above all, I hope you will find all of them musically satisfying.

John M. Feierabend

About Music
and Singing

All Things Shall Perish

All things shall per - ish from un - der the sky.
Him - mel und Er - de sie müs - sen ver - gehn;

Mu - sic a - lone shall live, Mu - sic a - lone shall live,
A - ber die Mus - i - ca, a - ber die Mus - i - ca,

Mu - sic a - lone shall live, nev - er to die.
A - ber die Mus - i - ca, bleibt be - stehen.

Auf, ihr Brüder (Get Up and Sing)

German

ME

Auf,   ihr   Brü - der,   auf   und   singt,

bis   es   im - mer   bes - ser,   im - mer   bes - ser   klingt.

General Translation

Up, you brother. Up, and sing until
it sounds even better.

Alternate Words

Ein sehr harter Winter ist,
wenn ein Wolf, ein Wolf,
ein Wolf den andern frißt.

General Translation

It is a very hard winter if a wolf eats
another wolf.

Come and Dance, Come and Sing

Antonio Caldara 1670-1736

M

Mit uns spring - et, mit uns singt,
Come and dance!___ Come and sing!

dass es im - mer schön - er klingt.
Let the world with laugh - ter ring.

La la la la la la la, la la la la la la la la,

la la la, la la la, la la la la la la.

Es Tönen die Lieder
(A Shepherd Sings the Song)

German

Es tö - nen die Lie - der, der Frü - ling kehrt wie - der

es spie - let— der— Hir - te auf sei - ner— Schal - mei

Tra - la - la - la - la - la - la - la,— tra - la - la - la - la - la - la - la.

General Translation

Songs are sounding, spring is returning, the shepherd plays his shawm.*

Tra la la la la la la la,
tra la la la la la la la.

*pipe or oboe

Freunde, Lasset uns Beim Zechen
(Friends, Forget the Cares that Bore Us)

Wolfgang Amadeus Mozart 1756-1791

Freun - de, las - set uns beim Ze - chen
Friends,   for - get the cares that   bore us.

wak - ker ei - ne Lan - ze bre - chen! Es leb' der
Come   and join the jol - ly   cho - rus.   A song of

Wein, die Lieb - ste mein! Drauf leer' sein Gläs - chen je - der
praise   to hap - py days.   Let us be mer - ry one and

aus. Mit euch ist gar nichts an - zu - fan - gen,
all. You sit so i - dly in your plac - es,

da sitzt ihr still wie Hop - fen - stan - gen.
with gloom - y looks up - on your fac - es.

Sie le - be hoch!   So schrei - et doch!
Come on re - joice!   And raise your voice!

Sie le - be hoch! So schrei - et doch, so schrei - et
To hap - py days a song of   praise, a song of

Jagdgesang (Hunting Song)

German

Tra - ra, das tönt wie Jagd - ge - sang, wie

wil - der und fröh - li - cher Hör - ner - klang, wie

Jagd - ge - sang, wie Hör - ner - klang: tra -

ra, tra - ra, tra - ra.

General Translation

Trara, that sounds like a hunting song,
Like a wild and cheerful sound of horns,
Like a hunting song, like the sound of horns.
Trara, trara, trara.

Lachend, Lachend (Laughing, Singing)

German

1. La - chend, la - chend, la - chend, la - chend
   Laugh - ing, sing - ing, laugh - ing, sing - ing,

2. Kommt der Som - mer ü - ber das Feld.
   Go the chil - dren o - ver the hill.

3. Ü - ber das — Feld kommt er la - chend, Ha - ha - ha,
   Fa - la - la - la - la - la - la - la, Ha - ha - ha;

4. La - chend ü - ber das Feld.
   Laugh - ing o - ver the hill.

General Translation

Laughing, laughing, laughing, laughing.
Comes the summer over the field.
Fa la la la la la la la la la ha ha ha,
Laughing over the field.

Let Us Endeavor

Let us en-deav-or To show that when-ev-er We

join in a song We can keep time to-geth-er.

Sing, Sing Together

Sing, sing to-geth-er, mer-ri-ly, mer-ri-ly sing;

Sing, sing to-geth-er, mer-ri-ly, mer-ri-ly sing;

Sing, sing, sing, sing.

Let us Sing Together

Let us sing to - geth - er, Let us sing to - geth - er,

One and all a joy - ous song. Let us sing to -

geth - er, One and all a joy - ous song.

Let us sing a - gain and a - gain, Let us sing a -

gain and a - gain, Let us sing a - gain and a - gain,

One and all a joy - ous song.

Nu, Nu, Nu, Nu (Let Us Sing and Be Happy)

Michael Praetorius 1571-1621

Nu,   nu, nu, nu,   nu schall   und sih   zu,

wat en Gsang is dat,   und wie kann dat sien,   drei

Stim   in ein,   singt   al - le   nach   mir.

Fa la don, di - ri don don don,   laßt uns freu - en und fröh - lich sein.

La   ri   don   di - ri   don   don   don.

General Translation

Nu, nu, nu, nu, nu,
Sing and watch what song is this.
How can it be, three voices as one?
Sing after me.
Fa la don, di ri don don don.
Let's be happy and cheerful.
La ri don diri don don.

Directions

Part 1

Begin in the key as written and cadence on the last note.

Part 2

Begin 2 beats later and a fourth lower and cadence 2 beats before the end.

Part 3

Begin 2 beats after and the interval of a fourth lower than Part 2 and cadence 5 beats before the end.

Now We are Met

Oh, Music, Sweet Music

Oh, mu - sic, sweet mu - sic, Thy prais - es we will

sing. We will tell of the pleas - ure and joy that you will

bring. Mu - sic mu - sic, joy that you will bring.

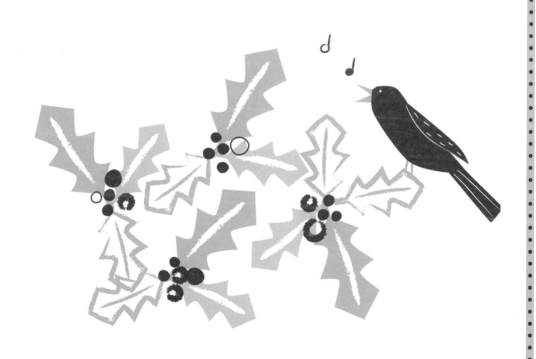

Sing With Thy Mouth

Thomas Ravenscroft 1582-1635

MD

1. Sing with thy mouth, sing with thy heart,

2. Like faith-ful friends, sing loath to de-part,

3. Though friends to-geth-er may not al-ways re-main, Yet

4. loath to de-part sing once a-gain.

The Bell Doth Toll

The bell doth toll, Its ech - oes roll, I
know the sound full well; I love its ring-ing, For it
calls to sing-ing, With its bim, bim, bim, bom, bell,
Bim, bom, bim, bom, bell.

Viva la Musica (Long Live Music)

Michael Praetorius 1571-1621

ME

1. Vi - va, vi - va la mu - si - ca,

2. Vi - va, vi - va la mu - si - ca,

3. Vi - va,_____ la mu - si - ca.

Animals and Critters

Ah, Poor Bird

Ah, poor bird take your flight,

Far a-bove the sor - rows of this sad night.

Benji Met a Bear

PHRYGIAN MODE

Ben - ji met a bear and the bear met Ben - ji, The

bear was bulg - y, The bulge was Ben - ji.

Grasshoppers Three

Grass - hop - pers three a - fid - dl - ing went,

Hey, Ho, nev - er be still. They

paid no mon - ey to - ward their rent, But

all day long with el - bow bent, They

fid - dled a tune called Ril - la - by Ril - la - by,

Fid - dled a tune called Ril - la - by Rill.

Little Bird Sits in a Holly Tree
(Opus 113 Number 3)

Johannes Brahms 1833-1897

M

1. Lit - tle bird sits in a hol - ly tree,
2. No, my love, that is no night - in - gale;

Sing - ing so hap - py and free;
No, my love that can - not be.

Tell me, what kind of a bird is___ he?
Night - in - gales do not like hol - ly___ trees.

A night - in - gale___ he must be.
Look for___ a___ ha - zel - nut tree.

Marjorie

Mar - jor - ie, go feed your black sow,

All on a mist - y morn - ing.

Come get your din - ner sow, come, come, come, Or

else you shall have nar - ry a crumb.

My Dame Has a Lame Tame Crane

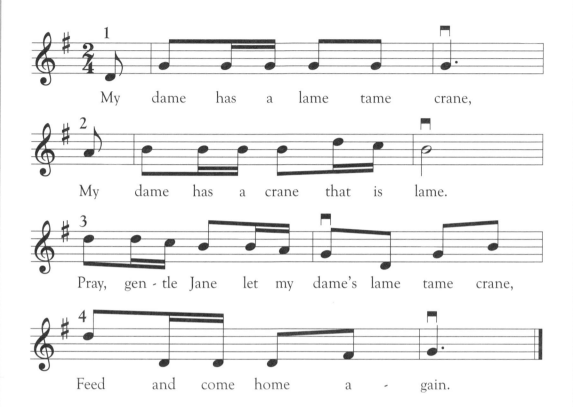

My dame has a lame tame crane,

My dame has a crane that is lame.

Pray, gen-tle Jane let my dame's lame tame crane,

Feed and come home a - gain.

> represents where the parts should cadence.

One Duck on a Pond

One duck on a pond, wib-ble, wob-ble.

Two ducks on a pond, wib-ble, wob-ble, wib-ble, wob-ble.

Three old la-dies go-ing to mar-ket,

Wib-bi-ly, wib-bi-ly wob-ble.

Three Blind Mice

Three blind mice, three blind mice,

See how they run, see how they run.— They

all ran af - ter the farm - er's wife. She

cut off their tails with a carv - ing knife. Did

ev - er you see such a sight in your life, As three blind mice?

The Spider to the Fly

"Will you come in - to my par - lor?"

said the spi - der to the fly.

"'Tis the pret - ti - est, snug - gest lit - tle par -

lor that ev - er you did spy."

"Not to - day, thanks, Mis - ter Long - shanks, I've

oth - er⎯ fish to fry!"

Why Shouldn't My Goose

Why should-n't my goose sing as well as thy goose?

When I paid for my goose twice as much as thine!

Friendship, Love, Peace and Conflict

Dona Nobis Pacem (Grant Us Peace)

Latin

M

Do - na no - bis pa - cem, pa - cem,

Do - na no - bis pa - cem,

Do - na no - bis — pa - cem,

Do - na — no - bis pa - cem.

Do - na no - bis pa - cem.

Do - na no - bis pa - cem.

Every White Will Have its Black

Ev - er - y white will have its black,

And ev - 'ry sweet its sour;

Most cru - el thorns will— ev - er lurk

Near - est the sweet - est flow'r.

Fie, Nay Prithee, John

Go to Joan Glover

Go to Joan Glo‑ver, and tell her I love her, and

at the mid of the moon I will come to her.

Here's a Health to All Them that We Love

1 Here's a health to all them that we love!____

2 Here's a health to all them that love us.____

3 Here's a health to all them that love those that love them,

4 That love those that love them that love us.____

Hyda, Hyda (Knowledge is Your Friend)

Hebrew

Hy - da, Hy - da, hy - di - de Hy - da, Hy - da, Hy - da, Hy - da!

Hy - da, hy - di - de Hy - da, Hy - da, Hy - da, Hy - da!

Hy - da, hy - di - de Hy - da, Hy - da, Hy - da, Hy - da!

Hy! Hy! Hy! Hy! Hy! Hy! Hy - da!

Jinkin the Jester

Jin - kin the jest - er was wont to make glee With

Jar - vis the jug - gler till an - gry was he. Then

Wil - kin the wise man did wise - ly fore - see, That

jug - gler and jest - er should gent - ly a - gree,

Hey down, down, down, down, der - ry

down, down, der - ry down, down.

*"Wont" is an old English word meaning simple minded desire.

Lo Yisa Goy (He Lifted a Nation)

Hebrew

M

Lo yi - sa goy___ el goy che - rev,

Lo___ yil - m' - du___ od mil - cha - ma.

Lo yi - sa goy___ el___ goy che___ rev,___

lo yil - m' - du___ od___ mil - cha - ma. Lo yi - sa goy___ el___

goy che___ rev,___ lo yil - m' - du___ od___ mil - cha - ma

General Translation

A nation shall not raise
a sword against a nation,
And they shall not learn
any more war.

Neemt mlj in de Hand
(Give to Me Your Hand)

Dutch

Neemt mlj in de hand, Hoort in 't kort ver-klar-en,
Give to me your hand! I will tell the sto-ry;

Wat er in ons land Al is we-der-var-en.
He-roes in our land, Tales of faith and glo-ry.

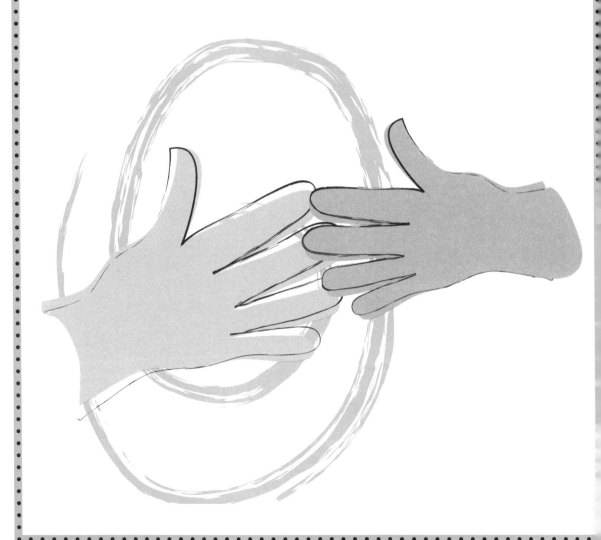

Our Door is Always Open

Our— door is al - ways o - pen

To our friends who pass this way,

We are al - ways glad— to— wel-come a friend

When he pass - es a - long our way.

O, Wollte doch der Mensch
(Oh, If Only Man)

Joseph Haydn 1732-1809

O, woll - te doch der Mensch des Men - schen Feind nicht

sein,— so— wär das mei - ste Weh noch un - be - kann - te

Pein.   O—   woll - te doch der

Mensch des Men - schen— Feind nicht sein, so—

wär— das mei - ste Weh noch un - be - kann - te

Pein. So wär das meis - te Weh— noch un - be - kann - te

Pein.—   So wär das meis - te Weh noch

un - be - kann - te Pein.——   So

wär —— das meis - te Weh,——   So wär das meis - te

Weh noch—— un - be - kann - te Pein.——

General Translation

Oh, if only man would not want to be the enemy of mankind,
then most of the pain would be unknown agony.

Pauper Sum Ego (I am So Poor)

Latin

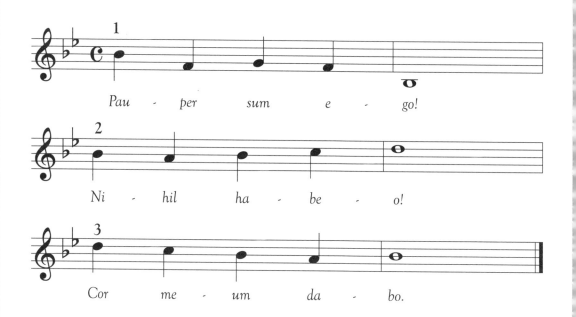

Pau - per sum e - go!

Ni - hil ha - be - o!

Cor me - um da - bo.

General Translation

I am so poor!
I have nothing!
I will give you my heart.

Rose, Rose, Rose, Rose

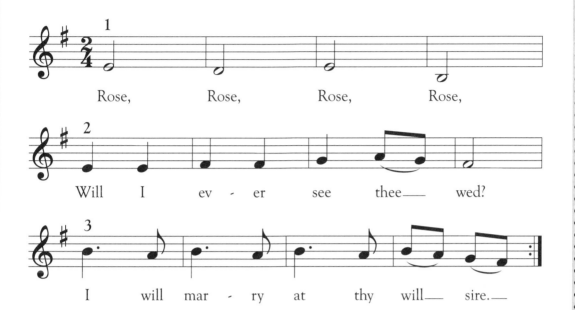

1 Rose, Rose, Rose, Rose,

2 Will I ev - er see thee— wed?

3 I will mar - ry at thy will— sire.—

Vine and Fig Tree

And ev - 'ry man 'neath his vine and

fig tree Shall live in peace and be un - a -

fraid. And ev - 'ry fraid. And in - to plow - shares

turn their swords Na - tions shall learn of war no more.

When I Go Home

Jamaica

When I go home I will tell my Ma - ma,

When I go home I will tell my Ma - ma,

When I go home I will tell my Ma - ma, Say

Ja - mai - ca girl won't leave me a - lone.

Willst du Immer Weiter Schweifen?
(Happiness is Always There)

Joseph Haydn 1732-1809

Willst du im - mer wei - ter schwei - fen?

Sieh, das Gu - te liegt so nah! ____

Ler - ne nur das Glück er -

grei - fen, denn das Glück ist im - mer

da, im - mer, im - mer da.

General Translation

Do you want to roam forever farther away?
Look, all good is so close!
Just learn to seize happiness,
because happiness is always there.

Humorous
and Clever

1, 3, 5, 8

1, 3, 5, 8, 7, 6, 5, 4, 3, 5, 2, 3,

4, sharp, 5 and the 8 is the same as the

1 but an oc - tave a - part; Try to learn it by heart.

A Ram Sam Sam

Morocco

A ram, sam, sam, A ram, sam, sam,

gu - li, gu - li, gu - li, gu - li, gu - li, ram, sam, sam.

A - ra - fi, a - ra - fi,

gu - li, gu - li, gu - li, gu - li, gu - li, ram, sam, sam.

Motions

During the first phrase pat on legs.

During the second and fourth phrases roll one hand over the other.

During the third phrase spread arms far apart and back twice.

Antonio Salieri Scherzo Canon

Composer: Antonio Salieri 1750-1825, lyrisist: Fritz Jöde 1887-1970

MD

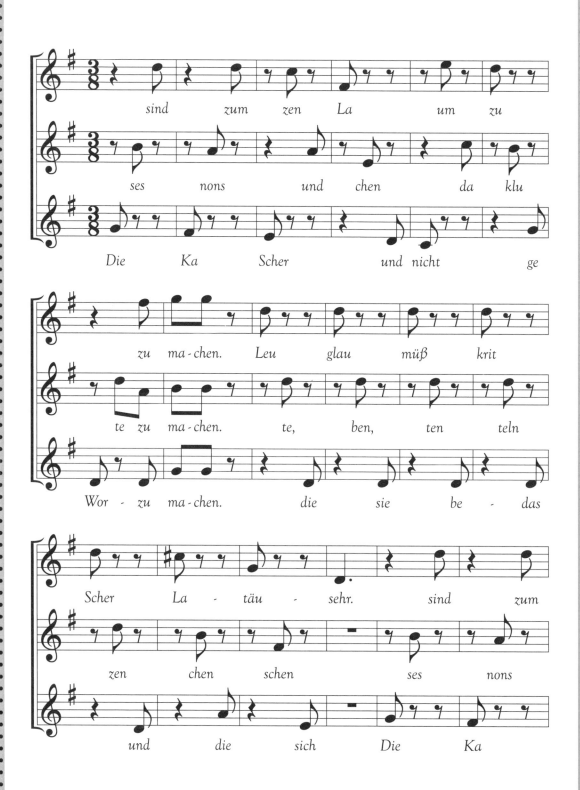

zen La - um zu zu ma - chen.

und chen da - klu - te zu ma - chen.

Scher und nicht ge Wor - zu ma - chen.

German Text

Dieses sind Kanons zum Scherzen und Lachen,
und nicht, um dazu kluge Worte zu machen.
Leute, die glauben, sie müßten bekritteln
das Scherzen und Lachen, die täuschen sich sehr.
Dieses sind Kanons zum Scherzen und Lachen,
und nicht, um dazu kluge Worte zu machen.

General Translation

These are canons for joking and laughing,
and not to make wise words.
People who believe they have to criticize
jokes and laughter are highly mistaken.

Black Socks

Black socks they nev-er get dir-ty the

lon-ger you wear 'em the strong-er they get. Some-times I

think I should wash 'em but some-thing keeps tell-ing me

"Don't wash 'em yet!" not yet, not yet, not yet.

Bubbling and Splashing

1 Bub-bling and splash-ing and foam-ing and dash-ing, With noise and with bus - tle, the brook rush-es by; But

2 si - lent and slow does the deep riv - er flow, On the smooth, glass - y sur - face re - flect - ing the sky. Thus

3 shal - low pre - tence bab-bles on with - out sense, While true know - ledge and wis - dom sit qui - et-ly by.

C Scale Canon

German

1. Ich bitt' dich, ich bitt' dich, schreib' mir die C - Ska-la auf!

2. do re mi fa sol la ti do   do ti la sol fa mi re do

3. mi fa sol la ti do re mi   mi re do ti la sol fa mi

General Translation

I beg you, write down a C Scale for me.

Das Hexen (The Witches Magic Square)

Joseph Haydn 1732-1809

1. Du mußt ver - stehn, aus Eins mach— Zehn, und— Zwei laß gehn, und Drei mach gleich, so bist du reich, bist du reich.

2. Aus Fünf und Sechs, so sagt die— Hex, mach— Sie - ben und Acht, so ist's voll - bracht, so ist's, ist's voll - bracht.

3. So ist's voll - bracht, und Neun ist— Eins, und— Zehn ist Keins, das ist das He - xen - ein - mal - eins, Ein - mal - eins.

General Translation

1. You have to understand;
   turn one into ten, let two be
   and make three the same.
   In that way you will be rich,
   you will be rich.

2. Turn five into six,
   so says the witch;
   come up with seven and eight.
   Then it is accomplished,
   then it is accomplished.

3. Then it is accomplished;
   and nine is one, and ten is none.
   That is the witches' 1-2-3.

Do, Re, Mi

Franz Joseph Haydn 1732-1809

Do, re, mi, mi, fa, fa, I am tired of

this sol - fa - ing And I know not what you're say - ing.

Duchess for Tea

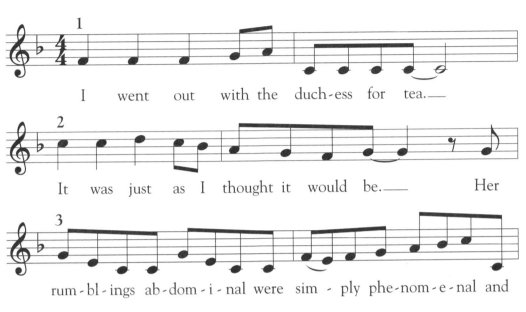

I went out with the duch-ess for tea.—

It was just as I thought it would be.— Her

rum-bl-ings ab-dom-i-nal were sim-ply phe-nom-e-nal and

eve-ry-one thought it was me.

Fester Sinn

Franz Joseph Haydn 1732-1809

1. Ein ein - zig bö - ses Weib lebt höch - stens in der Welt, nur
2. (Der Fels, an dem die Wut der Wo - gen sich zer - schellt, bist

schlimm, daß je - der seins für die - ses einz' - ge hält.
du, o fe - ster Sinn, der treu den Tap - fern hält.

Ein— ein - zig bö - ses— Weib, ein bö - ses
Der— Fels, an dem die— Wut der Wo - gen

Weib lebt höch - stens, lebt höch - stens in der Welt,
sich zer - schellt, bist du, o fe - ster Sinn, der treu

nur schlimm, daß je - der seins, daß je - der
den Tap - fern hält, bist du, o fe - ster

seins für die - ses einz' - ge hält.
Sinn, der treu den Tap - fern hält.)

This has the same melody with two different song settings. The two verses have nothing to do with each other.

General Translation 1

There is at most one wicked wife in the world, but it's sad that everyone considers his woman to be the only one.

General Translation 2

You are the rock that breaks the anger of the waves, it's you, the strong belief, that preserves the brave ones.

Haschet (Catch the Joy)

Franz Joseph Haydn 1732-1809

Ha - schet, ha - schet, hascht die Freu - de, wo sie weilt, ha - schet, ha - schet, denn schnell ist ihr Fit - tich! Ha-schet, ha-schet, haschet die Freu - de, wo sie weilt, ha - schet, denn schnell ist ihr Fit - tich, ihr Fit-tich, ihr Fit-tich, denn schnell, denn schnell ist ihr Fit - tich, schnell ist ihr Fit - tich, hascht, denn schnell ent - ei - let ihr Fit - tich!

General Translation

Catch the joy where it lingers,
catch it because its wings are fast!

Catch the joy where it lingers,
catch it because its wings are fast
and swiftly it will fly away!

One Bottle of Pop

One bot - tle of pop, two bot - tles of pop,

three bot - tles of pop, four bot - tles of pop,

Five bot - tles of pop, Six bot - tles of pop,

Se - ven bot - tles of pop, pop!

Don't throw your junk in my back - yard,

my back - yard, my back - yard, Don't throw your junk in

my back - yard, my back - yard's full.

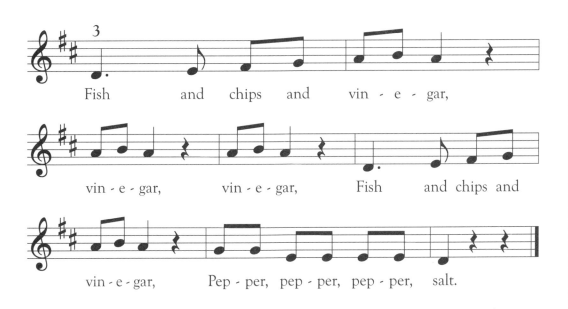

Fish and chips and vin - e - gar,

vin - e - gar, vin - e - gar, Fish and chips and

vin - e - gar, Pep - per, pep - per, pep - per, salt.

Toembai (A Nonsense Song)

Hebrew

1 Toem - bai, toem - bai, toem - bai, toem - bai,

toem - bai, toem - bai, toem - bai.

2 Tra la la, la la la la la, La la la la la la.

3 Tra la la la la, La la la la la, La la la la la, la.

When V and I Together Meet

When V and I to-geth-er meet, We make up six in House or Street;

Yet I and V may meet once more, And then we two can make but four.

But when that V from I am gone, al-las, poor I can make but one!

Meals and
Blessings

For Health and Strength

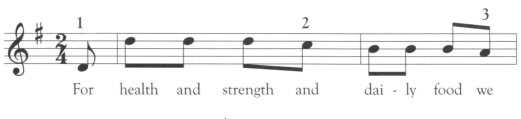

For health and strength and dai - ly food we

praise thy name O Lord.

For Thy Gracious Blessing

Two Part Canon

For Thy gra-cious bless-ings, For Thy won-d'rous word.

For Thy lov-ing kind-ness, We give thanks, Oh Lord.

Four Part Canon

For Thy gra-cious bless-ings, For Thy won-d'rous word.

For Thy lov-ing kind-ness, We give thanks, Oh Lord.

This may be sung as a two part or four part canon.

Praise and Thanksgiving

Praise and Thanks - giv - ing let ev' - ry - one bring

Un - to our Fa - ther for ev' - ry good thing.

All to - geth - er joy - ful - ly sing!

Morning
and Evening

Bona Nox (Good Night)

Wolfgang Amadeus Mozart 1756-1791

M

Bo - na nox, bist du rech - ter Ochs, Bo - na not - te, lie - be Lot - te, bonne nuit, pfui, pfui good— night, good— night. Heut' muss man so weit, gu - te Nacht, gu - te Nacht, 'swird höchs - te Zeit, gu - te Nacht. Schlaf', sei g'sund und werd recht ku - gel - rund.

This song is in German but also has Latin, Italian, French and English words.

General Translation

Good night, you are like an Ox.
Good night dear Lotte,
Good night, phooey, phooey,
Good night, Good night.
We have gone far today,
Good night, Good night.
It's time, good night, good night
To be sound as a bell and rest well.

Buon Giorno Mio Caro
(Good Morning, My Dear)

Italian

Buon gior-no mi-o ca-ro, Buon gior-no, mol-ti ba-ci.

Buon gior-no mi-o ca-ro, Buon gior-no, mol-ti ba-ci.

Buon gior-no mi-o ca-ro, Buon gior-no, mol-ti ba-ci.

General Translation

Good day, my dear,
Good day, many kisses.

Early As I Was Walking

Ear - ly as I was walk - ing, all on a

May morn - ing, I heard a bird sing.

Erwacht Ihr Schläferinnen
(Now Every Sleeper Waken)

German

Er - wacht, ihr Schlä - fe - rin - nen! Der Kuk-kuck hat ge
Now eve - ry sleep - er wak - en, the sun is in the

schrien Er - wa - chet, er - wa - chet, der
sky. Come rise——— come rise——— and

Kuk - kuck hat ge - schrien; Kuk - kuck, kuk -
hear the cuck - oo cry. Cuck - oo, Cuck -

kuck, kuk - kuck, kuk - kuck.
oo, Wake up, Be spry.

Farewell Dear

Fare - well dear; Peace be with thee;
When I'm gone Then— think of me.

Feierabend (Work is Finished)

German

Bim, bam, bim, bam! Horch, es sing't der Gloc-ken Ton
Din, don, din, don, C'est la clo-che du ma-tin,

von der Ar-beit sü-ßem Lohn: Fei-er-a-bend!
Qui sonne au le-ver du jour: Bon-jour, bon-jour!

Alternate English Text

Bim, bam, bim, bam!
Hear the bells, now work is done.
Telling us it's time for fun!
Feierabend!

General Translation

Bim, bam, bim, bam!
Listen, the sound of the bell
announces the sweet reward of work:
Closing time!

French Translation

Din, don, din, don!
It's the morning bell
that rings at the beginning of the day:
Good day! Good day!

Frère Jacques (Brother John)

French

Frè - re   Jac - ques,   Frè - re   Jac - ques,

Dor - mez - vous?   Dor - mez - vous?

Son - nez les ma - ti - nes,   Son - nez les ma - ti - nes,

Din,   dan,   don,   din,   dan,   don.

German Text

Bruder Jakob, Bruder Jakob,
schläfst du noch? schläfst du noch?
Hörst du nicht die Glocken,
Hörst du nicht die Glocken,
Ding, ding, dong, Ding, ding, dong.

General Translation

Brother John, Brother John,
Do you sleep? Do you sleep?
Hear the bells in the morning,
Hear the bells in the morning,
Ding, dong, ding, ding, dong, ding.

Gone to Bed is the Setting Sun

Gone to bed is the set - ting sun.

Night is com - ing and day is done. Whip-poor -

will, whip-poor-will has just— be - gun.

Good Night to You All

Good night to you all and sweet be your sleep;

May si - lence sur - round you, your slum - ber be deep.

Good night, good night, good night, good night.

Merrily, Merrily Greet the Morn

Mer - ri - ly, mer - ri - ly greet the morn,

Cheer - i - ly, cheer - i - ly sound the horn.

Hark to the ech - os! hear them play, O'er

hill and dale and far a - way!

Milha Bilou Loubi Shembel
(My Sweetest Darling)

Turkish

Mil - ha bi - lou lou - bi shem - bel,

mil - ha bi - lou lou - bi shem - bel,

mil - ha bi - lou lou - bi shem - bel,

mil - ha bi - lou lou - bi shem - bel.

Morning is Come

William H. Bradbury 1816-1868

Morn - ing is come. Night is a - way.

Rise with the sun——— and wel - come the day.

the book of canons

Nachtigallen Kanon (Nightingale Canon)

Franz Joseph Haydn 1732-1809

M

Al - les schwei - get, Nach - ti - gal - len

lock - en mit sü - ßen Me - lo - di - en

Trän - en ins Au - ge, Schwer - mut ins Herz,

lock - en mit sü - ßen Me - lo - di - en

Trän - en ins Au - ge, Schwer - mut ins Herz.

General Translation

Everything is quiet–
nightingales are bringing tears to the eyes
and melancholy in the heart
with their sweet melodies.

Now All the Woods Are Waking

Now all the woods are wak - ing, The
Now all the birds are chirp - ing, The

sun is rid - ing high. Wake
air is full of song. Wake

up, now! Get up, now! Be -
up, now! Get up, now! And

fore the dew is dry.
join the hap - py throng.

Now Comes the Hour for Peaceful Rest

Ludwig van Beethoven 1770-1827

1. Now comes the hour for peace - ful rest,
Oh, how blest! Peace - ful—— rest.

2. Ah—————————————— peace - ful rest.

3. Now comes the hour for peace - ful—— rest,
Oh, how blest!—— peace - ful rest.

O, How Lovely is the Evening

O how Love-ly is the eve-ning, Is the eve-ning;

When the bells are sweet-ly ring-ing, sweet-ly ring-ing.

Ding Dong, Ding Dong, Ding Dong.

Optional Dance

The class forms one large circle.

Phrase 1

Walk on the dotted quarter beat to the left.

Phrase 2

Walk on the dotted quarter note to the right.

Phrase 3

Swing arms; out, in, out, in, out, in.

Dance as a Round

Form three concentric circles. Sing and dance as a round. Perform the entire song two times. After the final time, each part repeats the last phrase until the last group has finished. On the last "dong," all children hum the last note as they slowly lift their arms in a large circle (forward, up and down). As they lower their arms, the humming fades out.

Shalom Chaverim (Goodbye, Friends)

Hebrew

Sha - lom cha - ve - rim, sha - lom cha - ve - rim, sha - lom, sha - lom. L' hit ra —— ot, l' hit re ot, sha - lom sha - lom.

General Translation

Goodbye, friends! Goodbye!
Good evening, friends!
Good evening!
Until we meet again!
Until we meet again!
Goodbye, friends! Goodbye!

Sing Me Another

Sing me an - oth - er be - fore we de - part,

Sing to the praise of our mu - si - cal art,

Sing, sing, sing, sing,

Do, do, do, sol, sol, sol, sol, sol, sol, do.

Welcome, Welcome Every Guest

Wel - come, wel - come ev' - ry guest.

Wel - come to our mu - sic fest.

Mu - sic is our on - ly____ cheer;

Fill both soul and____ rav - ished ear.

Sa - cred nine,____ teach us the mood.

Sweet - est notes to____ be ex - plored,

Soft - ly swell the trem - bling____ air,

To____ com - plete our____ con - cert fair.

Nature, Land
and Sea

A Boat, A Boat

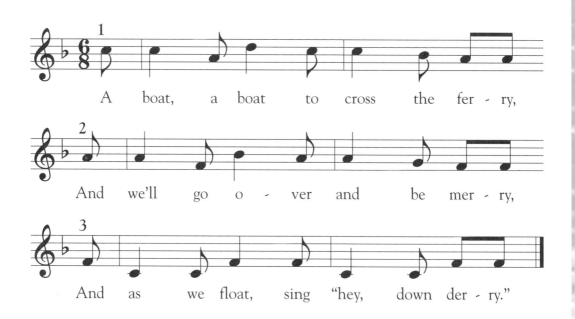

A boat, a boat to cross the fer - ry,

And we'll go o - ver and be mer - ry,

And as we float, sing "hey, down der - ry."

Above the Plain

A - bove the plain of gold and green,

A young boy's head is plain - ly seen;

A hu - ya, hu - ya, hu - ya - ya, Swift - ly flow - ing riv - er,

A hu - ya, hu - ya, hu - ya - ya, Swift - ly flow - ing riv - er.

Come Follow

John Hilton 1599-1657

Come, fol-low, fol-low, fol-low, fol-low, fol-low,

fol-low me. With-er shall I fol-low, fol-low, fol-low,

With-er shall I fol-low, fol-low thee? To the green-wood,

to the green-wood, to the green-wood green-wood tree.

Now I Walk in Beauty

Now I walk in beau-ty. Beau-ty is be-fore— me.

Beau-ty is be-hind me, A-bove— and be-low me.

I Love the Mountains

I love the moun-tains, I love the roll-ing hills,

I love the foun-tains, I love the daf-fo-dils,

I love the fi-re-side, when— the lights are low.

Boom-di-a-da, boom-di-a-da, Boom-di-a-da, boom-di-a-da,

Boom-di-a-da, boom-di-a-da, Boom-di-a-da, boom-di-a-da,

Last time

Boom-di-boom, boom.

Motions

In follow the leader fashion, children march with the beat while singing the song.

The leader should lead the group around in a twisting and turning line.

May be sung as a five part round.

On the River Flows

On the riv - er flows, strong, deep and si - lent.

On the riv - er flows, strong, deep and si - lent.

On to the might - y o - cean.

On to the might - y o - cean.

Rise Up, O Flame

Michael Praetorius 1571-1621

Rise up, O flame —————— By — thy — light

glow - ing, Show to us beau - ty, ——

Vi - sion ——— and joy.

'Round and 'Round

'Round and 'round the earth is turn - ing,

turn - ing, turn - ing 'round 'til morn - ing,

and from morn - ing 'round 'til night.

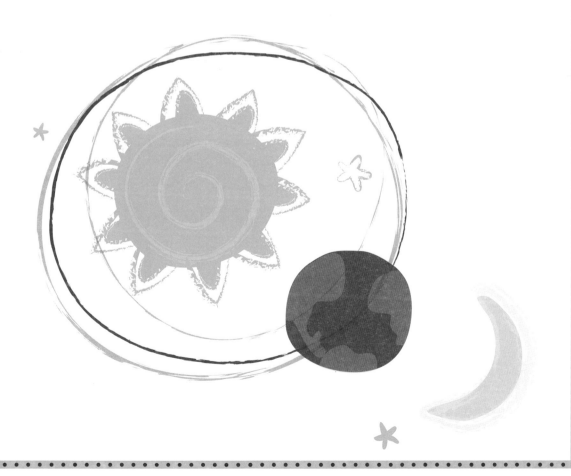

Row, Row, Row Your Boat

Row,   row,   row   your   boat,

gent - ly   down   the   stream.

Mer - ri - ly,   mer - ri - ly,   mer - ri - ly,   mer - ri - ly,

Life   is   but   a   dream.

We're On the Upward Trail

We're on the up - ward trail. We're on the up - ward trail.

Sing - ing, sing - ing, Ev - 'ry - bo - dy sing - ing, As we go.

We're on the up - ward trail. We're on the up - ward trail.

Sing - ing, sing - ing, Ev - 'ry - bo - dy sing - ing, Home - ward bound.

White Coral Bells

Can be sung as a four part canon one measure apart

1

White cor - al bells up - on a slen - der stalk,
Oh, don't you wish that you could hear them ring?

2

Lil - ies of the val - ley deck my gar - den walk.
That will hap - pen on - ly when the an - gels sing.

On Death
and Dying

Das Licht ist Mir Erloschen
(The Light has Faded)

D

Antonio Salieri 1750-1825

Das Licht ist mir er - lo - schen; ich weiß nicht, wo ich

bin. Ich wen - de mich hin - auf, ich wen - de mich hin -

ab: Sagt, wo - hin? Sagt, wo - hin? Das Licht ist mir er -

lo - schen; ich weiß nicht, wo ich bin. Ich wen - de mich hin -

auf, ich wen - de mich hin - ab: Sagt,— wo -

hin? Sagt,— wo - hin? Ach, das Licht ist mir er -

lo - schen, sagt, wo - hin? Ich

weiß nicht, wo ich bin: Sagt, wo - hin? Sagt, wo - hin?

General Translation

The light has faded for me;
I don't know where I am.
I am turning upwards,
and I am turning downwards.
Tell me: where?

Death is a Long, Long Sleep

Death is a long, _____ long ___

sleep; Sleep is a short re - treat from

life that soothes our cares as death brings still-ness af - ter

strife; Death is a long, long sleep.

Here Lies Jack Chill

Franz Joseph Haydn 1732-1809

Here lies Jack Chill with his wife——

Jill. A—— wretch - ed man was

Chill. And what———— then, and

what then was Jill?

 indicates a point to cadence.

If You Trust

Charles Frederick Lampe 1740-1780

If you trust be - fore you try, You

may re - pent be - fore you die, You

may re - pent be - fore you die.

Old Abram Brown

Old A - bram Brown is dead and gone,

you'll nev - er see him more.

He used to wear a long brown coat

that but - toned down be - fore.

Under the Stone

Henry Purcell 1638-1695

Un - der the stone lies Ga - bri-el John, in the

year of our Lord, one thou - sand and one.

Cov - er his head with turf—— or stone. 'Tis all

one, 'tis all one, with turf or stone, 'tis all one.

Pray for the soul of gen - tle—— John if you

please you may or let—— it a - lone, 'tis all one.

People, Places, and Things

Ceciderunt in Profundum
(Fallen into the Depths)

Georg Philipp Telemann 1681-1767

Ce - ci - de - runt in pro - fun - dum
sum - mus A - ri - sto - te - les, Pla - to et Eu - ri - pi - des.

Ce - ci - de - runt, ce - ci - de - runt in pro - fun - dum
sum - mus A - ri - sto - te - les, Pla - to et Eu - ri - pi - des.

Ce - ci - de - runt in pro - fun - dum
sum - mus A - ri - sto - te - les, Pla - to et Eu - ri - pi - des.

General Translation

Aristotle, Plato, and Euripides,
all together, have fallen into the depths.

Chairs to Mend

Chairs to mend, old chairs to mend! Mack - er - el, fresh

Mack - er - el! An - y old rags, an - y old rags?

Come To the Top of the Path

Come to the top of the path in the gar - den,

Look how the sails are turn - ing up so

Down a - gain and down a - gain the

There you'll see the mill.

fast up - on the hill and fall - ing—

ground they touch un - til.

Motions

During the first phrase take quick steps around in a circle. During the
second phrase extend arms straight out and sway from side to side. During
the third phrase begin with hands above head and slowly lower hands to
the ground by the end. Perform as a canon in three concentric circles.

Hark! Roars the Bellows

Gustav Holst 1874-1934

Hark! roars the bel - lows, blast on blast, The soot - y smith - y___ jars,___ And fire - sparks ris - ing far and fast, Are fad - ing with the___ stars. All day for us the smith shall stand, Be - side that flash - ing forge; All day for us his heav - y hand, The groan - ing an - vil scourge. From far off hills the pant - ing team, For us is draw - ing___ near; For

us the rafts - men down the stream, Their is - land bar - ges steer. Rings out for us the axe - man's stroke In for - ests old and still, For us the cen - tu - ry cir - cled oak, Falls crash - ing down his hill.

Have You Seen the Ghost of John

AEOLIAN MODE

1 Have you seen the— ghost of John?

2 Long white bones with the skin all gone.———

3 Ooo - ooo - ooo - ooo.

4 Would-n't it be chil - ly with no skin on?

Hey, Ho, Nobody Home

Hey, Ho, no - bod - y home.

Meat nor drink nor mon - ey have I none.

Yet, I will be mer - ry, —

See "Rose, Rose" on page 51 for alternate words.

Little Tom Tinker

1 Lit - tle Tom Tink - er, sat on a clink - er and

2 he be - gan to cry, **3** "Ma!_____ Ma!_____

4 Poor lit - tle in - no - cent I."

Derry Ding Dong Dason

Make New Friends

Martin, Lieber Herre (Martin, Dear Sir)

German

DORIAN MODE

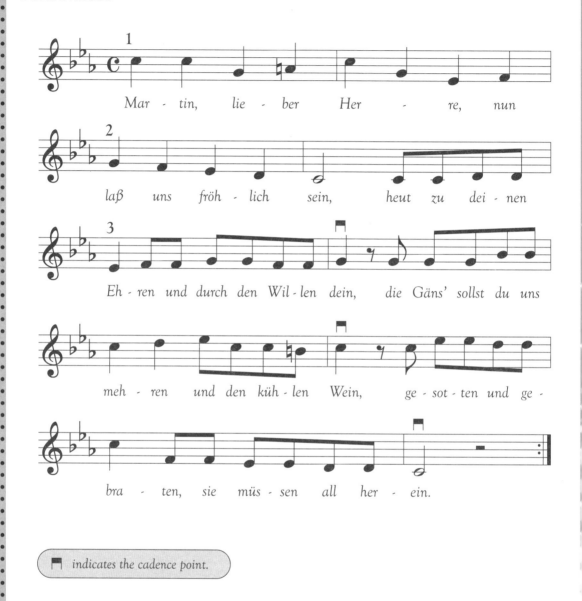

Mar - tin, lie - ber Her - re, nun

laß uns fröh - lich sein, heut zu dei - nen

Eh - ren und durch den Wil - len dein, die Gäns' sollst du uns

meh - ren und den küh - len Wein, ge - sot - ten und ge -

bra - ten, sie müs - sen all her - ein.

 indicates the cadence point.

General Translation

Martin, dear sir, let's be cheerful.
Today in your honor and by your will,
you shall increase the number of geese
and the amount of wine.
Boiled and fried, they must be available.

Scotland's Burning

Scot - land's burn - ing, Scot - land's burn - ing,

Look out! Look out!

Fire! Fire! Fire! Fire!

Pour on wa - ter, Pour on wa - ter.

The hun-ter winds his bu-gle horn, To horse! To horse! Hal-loo! Hal-loo!— The fier-y cours-ers snuff the morn, While throng-ing serf— and lord pur-sue. The ea-ger pack in cou-ples freed Dash thro' the brook, the briar, the brake,— While an-s'ring horn and hound and steed The for-est ech-oes start-ling wake. Up springs from yon-der tan-gled thorn A

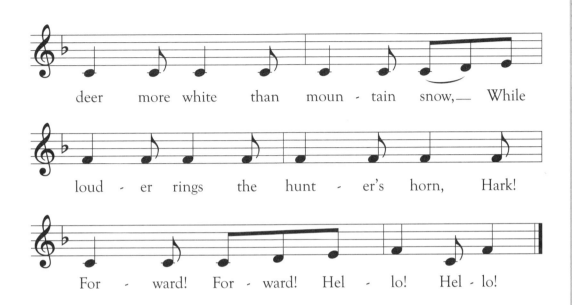

deer   more white   than   moun - tain snow,— While

loud - er rings   the   hunt - er's horn,   Hark!

For - ward! For - ward! Hel - lo!   Hel - lo!

Two Lawyers

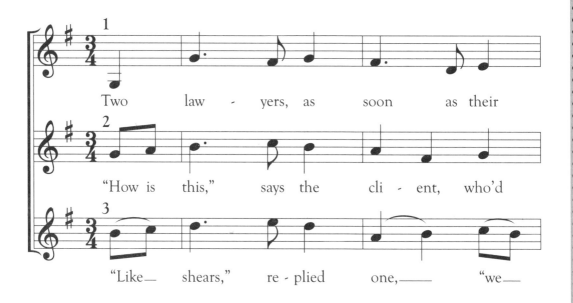

Two law - yers, as soon as their

"How is this," says the cli - ent, who'd

"Like— shears," re - plied one,——— "we—

con - test was o'er, shook hands and were

lost, "tell me how You two are such

law - yers, so keen, Ne'er cut our own

just   as good   friends   as be - fore.

friends who   were   such   foes just now?"

selves, _____   but__ what   is be - tween."

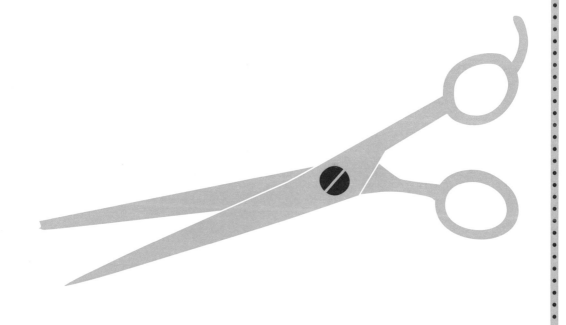

The Little Bell at Westminster

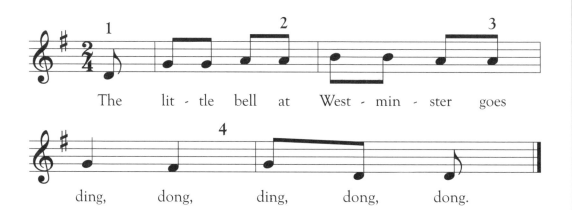

The lit - tle bell at West - min - ster goes

ding, dong, ding, dong, dong.

White Sand and Gray Sand

White sand and gray sand;

Who'll buy my white sand?

Who'll buy my gray sand?

We Merry Minstrels

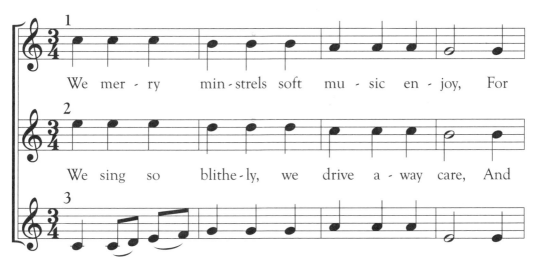

We mer-ry min-strels soft mu-sic en-joy, For

We sing so blithe-ly, we drive a-way care, And

Then hail sweet sci-ence, hail, hail, hev'n-ly sound! No

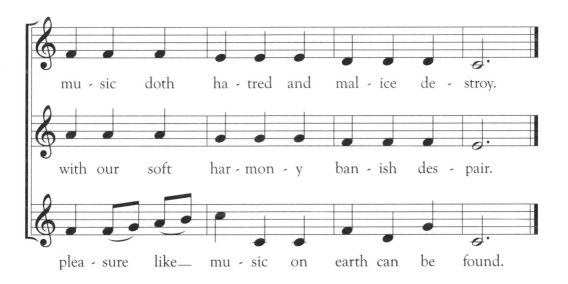

mu-sic doth ha-tred and mal-ice de-stroy.

with our soft har-mon-y ban-ish des-pair.

plea-sure like— mu-sic on earth can be found.

Where is John?

Bedřich Smetana 1824-1884

1 Where is John? The old red hen has left her pen.

2 Where is John? The cows are in the corn a - gain. Oh,

3 John!

Willie, Willie, Will

Johannes Brahms 1833-1897

Wil - lie, Wil - lie, Will, a man is com - ing,

Wil - lie, Wil - lie, Will, what brings he here?

Wil - lie, Wil - lie, Will,— fine— sug - ar wa - fers.

Wil - lie, Wil - lie, Will, they're for a child that's dear.

Sing each note as if marked staccato.

Young Rider

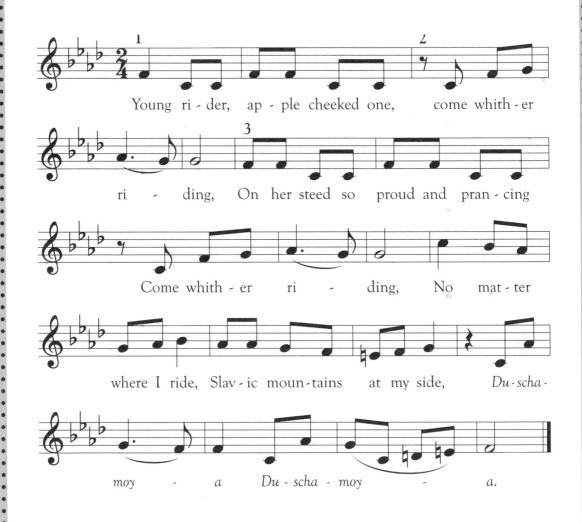

Young ri - der, ap - ple cheeked one, come whith - er

ri - ding, On her steed so proud and pran - cing

Come whith - er ri - ding, No mat - ter

where I ride, Slav - ic moun - tains at my side, Du - scha -

moy - a Du - scha - moy - a.

Duschamoya means "little sweetheart" in Russian.

Sacred
and Latin

Alleluia

Wolfgang Amadeus Mozart 1756-1791

Al - le - lu - ia,

Al - - - - -

- - le - lu - ia,

Al - - - le - lu - ia,

Al - le - lu - ia. A -

- men Al - le - lu - ia.

All Praise to Thee

Thomas Tallis 1505-1585

All praise to thee, my God, this night,

For all the bless - ings of the light;

Keep me, oh, keep me, King of Kings,

Be - neath Thine own Al - might - y wings.

Jubilate Deo (Sing Joyfully to God)

Latin

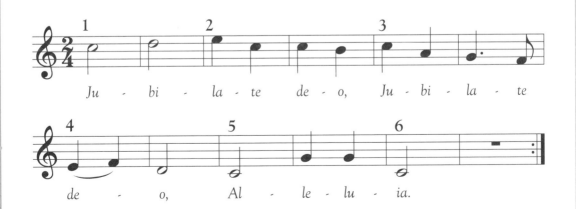

Ju - bi - la - te de - o, Ju - bi - la - te

de - o, Al - le - lu - ia.

Ave Maria

Wolfgang Amadeus Mozart 1756-1791

A - ve Ma - ri - a, A - ve— Ma - ri - a! A - ve, A - ve— Ma - ri - a! A - ve Ma - ri - a Ma - ri - a, A - ve, A - ve Ma - ri - a, A - ve, A - ve!

By the Waters of Babylon

By the wa-ters, by the wa-ters, by the wa-ters of

Ba - by-lon. We sat down and wept,— and

wept— for thee, Zi - on. We re - mem - ber,

we re -mem - ber, we re -mem - ber thee, Zi - on.

Cantate Domino (Sing to the Lord)

Adam Gumpelzhaimer 1559-1625

DORIAN MODE

Can - ta - - - te____

Do - - - mi - no can - ti -

cum no - vum, can -

ti - cum____ no - vum, can - ti - cum no - vum

General Translation

Sing to the Lord a new song.

Christmas is Coming

1
Christ - mas is com - ing the goose is get - ting fat.
If you've no pen - ny, a ha' pen - ny will do.

2
Please to put a pen - ny in the old man's hat.
If you have no ha' pen - ny, then God bless you.

3
Please to put a pen - ny in the old man's hat.
If you have no ha' pen - ny, then God bless you.

A ha' penny is a half penny.

Da Pacem Domine (Give Peace Lord)

Latin

Da pa - cem, Do - mi - ne, da pa - cem,

Do - mi - ne, in di - e - bus nos - tris.

General Translation

Give peace, Lord, in our days.

Kyrie, Kyrie, Eleison (Lord, Have Mercy)

Latin

Ky - ri - e, ky - ri - e, e - le - i - son.

Ky - ri - e, ky - ri - e, e - le - i - son.

Ky - ri - e, ky - ri - e,— e - lei - son.

Ehre sei Gott in der Höhe
(Glory to God in the Highest)

Ludwig Ernst Gebhardt 1787-1862

1. Eh - re sei Gott in der Hö - he!
   Glo - ry to God in the high - est,

2. Frie - de auf Er - den, auf Er - den und den
   Hal - le - lu - jah, Hal - le - lu - jah, And

3. Men - schen ein Wohl - ge - fal - len. A -
   peace on the earth, good will to all men. A -

4. men. A - men.
   men, A - men.

Gaudeamus (Let Us Rejoice Today)

1 Gau-de-a-mus, Gau-de-a-mus Gau-de-a-mus ho-di-e!

Gau-de-a-mus, Gau-de-a-mus ho-di-e!

2 Gau - de - a - mus, Gau - de -

a - mus ho - di - e! **3** Gau - de - a - mus, Gau - de -

a - mus, Gau - de - a - mus ho - di - e! Ho - di - e!

Geht, Hinin Alle Welt (Go, Out Into the World)

Adam Gumpelzhaimer 1559-1625

MD

Geht,——— hin - in al - le Welt, leh -

ret al - le Völ - ker und tau - fet sie, und tau - fet

sie im Na - men des Va - ters und des Sohns———

— und des Hei - li - gen Gei - stes, und des Hei -

li - gen Gei - stes, Gei - stes.

▛ *represents the cadence point.*

General Translation

Go out into the world,
teach and baptize all people,
baptize them in the name of the Father,
and the Son, and the Holy Spirit.

Hashivenu (Turn Us to You, O God)

Hebrew

Ha - shi ve - nu,

Ha - shem e - le - cha,

V' - na shu - va,

V' - na shu - va,

Ka - desh, ka - desh ya

me - nuk' ke - dem.

General Translation

Turn us to You, O God;
and we shall return.
Renew our days as of old.

Hava Nashira (Let Us Sing a Song of Praise)

Hebrew

1
Ha - va - na - shi - ra. Shir al - le - lu - ia!

2
Ha - va na - shi - ra. Shir al - le - lu - ia!

3
Ha - va na - shi - ra. Shir al - le - lu - ia!

General Translation

Let us sing a song of praise.
Sing alleluia!

Like As a Father

Luigi Cherubini 1760-1842

1. Like as a fa - ther pit - ieth his—

2. fear— Him; Like as a fa - ther

3. Like as a fa - ther pit - ieth his

chil - dren. So the Lord has mer - cy,

pit - i - eth, pit - ieth his chil - dren,

chil - dren. So the Lord has

So the Lord has mer - cy, So the Lord has

The Lord has mer - cy, the Lord has

mer - cy, the Lord has mer - cy on

mer - cy on them that fear, on them that

mer - cy on them that fear Him.

them ———————— that fear Him.

Masters in This Hall

Non Nobis Domine (Not to Us, Lord)

William Byrd 1540-1623

Directions

Part 2 begins the interval of a fourth below Part 1.

Part 3 begins on the same pitch as Part 1.

After Singing Twice:

Part 1 ends at A.

Part 2 ends at B.

Part 3 ends at C.

General Translation

O Lord, not to us but to your name give glory.

Sanctus (Holy)

Jacobus Clemens non Papa 1510-1556

San - (ctus)* _____

ctus, San - - -

- ctus, San - - -

(ctus) _____

_____ ctus, San - ctus.

Directions

The syllables in parentheses* are sung only at the final cadence.

The fermatas indicate the final cadences only and should be disregarded otherwise.

Verbum Domini (The Word of the Lord)

Adam Gumpelzhaimer 1559-1625

General Translation

The word of the Lord
endures forever.

When Jesus Wept

AEOLIAN MODE

When Je - sus wept___ the fall - ing tear

In mer - cy flow'd___ be - yond all bound;

When Je - sus groan'd a trem - bling fear

Seized all___ the guil - ty world___ a - round.

Seasons

Beau Printemps (Beautiful Spring)

Roland de Lassus 1532 - 1594

1. Dis - moi, beau prin - temps, pour qui sont ces fleurs et ces chan - sons?

2. La lu - ne blan - che dans l'e - tang,

3. Les nids - blot - tis - dans les tail - lis

4. De ta beau - té, de tes par - fums ne nous las - sons.

General Translation

Tell me, beautiful spring, for whom are the flowers and songs? The white moon in the pond, the nests tucked into the thickets of your beauty, we will not tire of their smell.

Die Blumen (Flowers)

German

Die Blu-men und das Laub die fal - len in den

Staub, und al - ler Erd - en Herr - lich-keit, das

bleibt nur ei - ne kur - ze— Zeit, und muß ver -

geh'n, und muß———— ver - geh'n.

General Translation

Flowers and leaves fall into the dust,
and all earthly glory remains only for a short time,
and must perish, and must perish.

Flow'rs are Dying

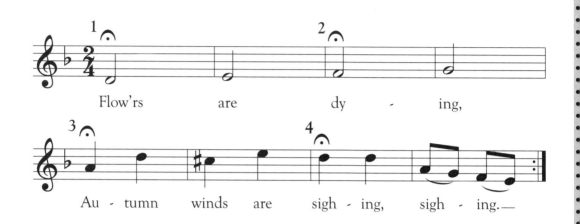

Flow'rs are dy - ing,

Au - tumn winds are sigh - ing, sigh - ing.—

Nicht Länger ist Winter (It's No Longer Winter)

German

ME

Nicht län - ger—— ist Win - ter, schon

grü - net—— der Hain,—— schon la - det—— der

Früh - ling zum Tan - ze uns ein.——

General Translation

It's no longer winter,
The grove is already blossoming,
Spring is asking us for a dance.

Sumer is Icumen In

This canon is the oldest known secular piece of music in print.

Willkommen, Lieber Schöner Mai
(We Welcome Lovely Month of May)

Franz Schubert 1757-1828

M

Will - kom - men, lie - ber schö - ner Mai, dir
We wel - come love - ly month of May, With

tönt___ der Vö - gel Lob - ge - sang.
wren___ and rob - in's roun - de - lay.

Will - kom - men, lie - ber schö - ner Mai, dir
We wel - come love - ly month of May, With

tönt___ der Vö - gel Lob - ge - sang.
wren___ and rob - in's roun - de - lay.

Will - kom - men, lie - ber schö - ner Mai, dir
We wel - come love - ly month of May, With

tönt___ der Vö - gel Lob - ge - sang.
wren___ and rob - in's roun - de - lay.

Songs Without Words

Great songs to sing with solfege syllables!

Caldara Canon #1

Antonio Caldara 1670-1736

Caldara Canon #2

Antonio Caldara 1670-1736

Cherubini Canon #1

Luigi Cherubini 1760-1842

Cherubini Canon #2

Luigi Cherubini 1760-1842

Crab Canon

Johann Sebastian Bach 1685-1750

the book of canor

Directions

This canon can be sung forwards or backwards,
either right side up or upside down.

Haydn Crab Canon

Franz Joseph Haydn 1732 - 1809

Directions

This canon can be sung forwards or backwards,
either right side up or upside down.

Minor Canon

Schubert Canon

Franz Schubert 1757-1828

Indexes

Songs by Title

1, 3, 5, 8, 56
A Boat, A Boat, 102
A Ram Sam Sam, 57
Above the Plain, 103
Ah, Poor Bird, 26
All Praise to Thee, 145
All Things Shall Perish, 8
Alleluia, 144
Antonio Salieri Scherzo Canon, 58
Auf, ihr Brüder (Get Up and Sing), 9
Ave Maria, 146
Beau Printemps (Beautiful Spring), 164
Bell Doth Toll, The, 23
Benji Met a Bear, 27
Black Socks, 60
Bona Nox (Good Night), 80
Bubbling and Splashing , 61
Buon Giorno Mio Caro
   (Good Morning My Dear), 82
By the Waters of Babylon, 147
C Scale Canon, 62
Caldara Canon # 1, 172
Caldara Canon # 2, 173
Cantate Domino (Sing to the Lord), 148
Ceciderunt in Profundum
   (Fallen into the Depths), 122
Chairs to Mend, 124
Cherubini Canon # 1, 174
Cherubini Canon # 2, 175
Christmas is Coming, 149
Come and Dance, Come and Sing, 10
Come Follow, 104
Come to the Top of the Path, 125
Crab Canon, 176
Da Pacem Domine (Give Peace Lord), 150
Das Hexen (The Witches Magic Square), 63
Das Licht ist Mir Erloschen
   (The Light has Faded), 114
Death is a Long, Long Sleep, 116
Derry Ding Dong Dason, 131
Die Blumen (Flowers), 165
Do, Re, Mi, 64
Dona Nobis Pacem (Grant Us Peace), 38
Duchess for Tea, 65

Early As I Was Walking, 83
Ehre sei Gott in der Höhe
   (Glory to God in the Highest), 151
Erwacht Ihr Schlaferin
   (Now Every Sleeper Waken), 84
Es Tönen Die Lieder
   (A Shepherd Sings the Song), 11
Every White Will Have its Black, 39
Farewell Dear, 85
Feierabend (Work is Finished), 86
Fester Sinn, 66
Fie, Nay Prithee, John, 40
Flow'rs Are Dying, 166
For Health and Strength, 76
For thy Gracious Blessing, 77
Frère Jacques (Brother John), 87
Freunde, Lasset uns Beim Zechen
   (Friends, Forget the Cares that Bore Us), 12
Gaudeamus (Let Us Rejoice Today), 152
Geht, Hinin Alle Welt
   (Go Out Into the World), 153
Go to Joan Glover, 41
Gone to Bed is the Setting Sun, 88
Good Night to You All, 89
Grasshoppers Three, 28
Hark! Roars the Bellows, 126
Haschet (Catch the Joy), 68
Hashivenu (Turn Us to You, O God), 154
Hava Nashira
   (Let Us Sing a Song of Praise), 155
Have You Seen the Ghost of John, 128
Haydn Crab Canon, 178
Here Lies Jack Chill, 117
Here's a Health to All Them that We Love, 42
Hey, Ho, Nobody Home, 129
Hunter, The, 134
Hyda, Hyda (Knowledge is Your Friend), 43
I Love the Mountains, 106
If You Trust, 118
Jagdgesang (Hunting Song), 14
Jinkin the Jester, 44
Jubilate Deo (Sing Joyfully to God), 145
Kyrie, Kyrie, Eleison (Lord, Have Mercy), 150
Lachend, Lachend (Laughing, Singing), 15

Let Us Endeavor, 16
Let Us Sing Together, 17
Like As a Father, 156
Little Bell at Westminster, The, 138
Little Bird Sits in a Holly Tree, 29
Little Tom Tinker, 130
Lo Yisa Goy (He Lifted a Nation), 45
Make New Friends, 131
Marjorie, 30
Martin, Lieber Herre (Martin, Dear Sir), 132
Masters in This Hall, 158
Merrily, Merrily Greet the Morn, 90
Milha Bilou Loubi Shembel
    (My Sweetest Darling), 91
Minor Canon, 179
Morning is Come , 92
My Dame Has a Lame Tame Crane, 31
Nachtigallen Kanon (Nightingale Canon), 93
Neemt mlj in de Hand
    (Give to Me Your Hand), 46
Nicht Länger ist Winter
    (It's No Longer Winter), 167
Non Nobis Domine (Not to Us, Lord), 159
Now All the Woods Are Waking, 94
Now Comes the Hour for Peaceful Rest, 95
Now I Walk in Beauty, 105
Now We Are Met, 20
Nu, Nu, Nu, Nu
    (Let Us Sing and Be Happy), 18
O, How Lovely is the Evening, 96
O, Wollte doch der Mensch
    (Oh, If Only Man), 48
Oh, Music, Sweet Music, 21
Old Abram Brown, 119
On the River Flows, 107
One Bottle of Pop, 70
One Duck on a Pond, 32
Our Door is Always Open, 47
Pauper Sum Ego (I am So Poor), 50

Praise and Thanksgiving, 78
Rise Up, O Flame, 108
Rose, Rose, Rose, Rose, 51
Round and Round, 109
Row, Row, Row Your Boat, 110
Sanctus (Holy), 160
Schubert Canon, 180
Scotland's Burning, 133
Shalom Chaverim (Goodbye, Friends), 97
Sing Me Another, 98
Sing with Thy Mouth, 22
Sing, Sing Together, 16
Spider to the Fly, The, 34
Sumer is Icumen In, 168
Three Blind Mice, 33
Toembai (A Nonsense Song), 72
Two Lawyers, 136
Under the Stone, 120
Verbum Domini (The Word of the Lord), 161
Vine and Fig Tree, 52
Viva la Musica (Long Live Music), 24
We Merry Minstrels, 139
We're On the Upward Trail, 111
Welcome, Welcome Every Guest, 99
When I Go Home, 53
When Jesus Wept, 162
When V and I Together Meet, 73
Where is John, 140
White Coral Bells, 112
White Sand and Gray Sand, 138
Why Shouldn't My Goose, 35
Willie, Willie, Will, 141
Willst, du lmmer Weiter Schweifen
    (Happiness is Always There), 54
Willkommen, Lieber Schöner Mai
    (We Welcome Lovely Month of May), 170
Young Rider, 142

Songs by Difficulty Level

Easy

26 Ah, Poor Bird
35 Why Shouldn't My Goose
76 For Health and Strength
77 For thy Gracious Blessing
87 Frère Jacques (Brother John)
92 Morning is Come
102 A Boat, A Boat
110 Row, Row, Row Your Boat
124 Chairs to Mend

130 Little Tom Tinker
131 Make New Friends
133 Scotland's Burning
138 Little Bell at Westminster, The
138 White Sand and Gray Sand
179 Minor Canon

Medium Easy

8 All Things Shall Perish
9 Auf, ihr Brüder (Get Up and Sing)

the book of canon

14 Jagdgesang (Hunting Song)
15 Lachend, Lachend (Laughing, Singing)
16 Let Us Endeavor
16 Sing, Sing Together
17 Let Us Sing Together
23 Bell Doth Toll, The
24 Viva la Musica (Long Live Music)
27 Benji Met a Bear
31 My Dame Has a Lame Tame Crane
32 One Duck on a Pond
33 Three Blind Mice
34 Spider to the Fly, The
41 Go to Joan Glover
47 Our Door is Always Open
50 Pauper Sum Ego (I am So Poor)
51 Rose, Rose, Rose, Rose
56 1, 3, 5, 8
57 A Ram Sam Sam
60 Black Socks
62 C Scale Canon
64 Do, Re, Mi
70 One Bottle of Pop
72 Toembai (A Nonsense Song)
78 Praise and Thanksgiving
84 Erwacht Ihr Schlaferin
   (Now Every Sleeper Waken)
85 Farewell Dear
86 Feierabend (Work is Finished)
88 Gone to Bed is the Setting Sun
89 Good Night to You All
90 Merrily, Merrily Greet the Morn
91 Milha Bilou Loubi Shembel
   (My Sweetest Darling)
94 Now All the Woods Are Waking
96 O, How Lovely is the Evening
97 Shalom Chaverim (Goodbye, Friends)
98 Sing Me Another
103 Above the Plain
104 Come Follow
106 I Love the Mountains
107 On the River Flows
108 Rise Up, O Flame
111 We're On the Upward Trail
112 White Coral Bells
119 Old Abram Brown
128 Have You Seen the Ghost of John
129 Hey, Ho, Nobody Home
131 Derry Ding Dong Dason
140 Where is John
145 Jubilate Deo (Sing Joyfully to God)
149 Christmas is Coming
150 Da Pacem Domine (Give Peace Lord)
166 Flow'rs Are Dying

167 Nicht Länger ist Winter
   (It's No Longer Winter)

Medium

10 Come and Dance, Come and Sing
11 Es Tönen Die Lieder
   (A Shepherd Sings the Song)
20 Now We Are Met
21 Oh, Music, Sweet Music
28 Grasshoppers Three
29 Little Bird Sits in a Holly Tree
30 Marjorie
38 Dona Nobis Pacem (Grant Us Peace)
39 Every White Will Have its Black
42 Here's a Health to All Them that We Love
43 Hyda, Hyda (Knowledge is Your Friend)
45 Lo Yisa Goy (He Lifted a Nation)
46 Neemt mlj in de Hand
   (Give to Me Your Hand)
52 Vine and Fig Tree
53 When I Go Home
54 Willst, du lmmer Weiter Schweifen
   (Happiness is Always There)
61 Bubbling and Splashing
63 Das Hexen (The Witches Magic Square)
65 Duchess for Tea
80 Bona Nox (Good Night)
82 Buon Giorno Mio Caro
   (Good Morning My Dear)
83 Early As I Was Walking
93 Nachtigallen Kanon (Nightingale Canon)
95 Now Comes the Hour for Peaceful Rest
99 Welcome, Welcome Every Guest
109 Round and Round
116 Death is a Long, Long Sleep
117 Here Lies Jack Chill
118 If You Trust
125 Come to the Top of the Path
132 Martin, Lieber Herre (Martin, Dear Sir)
134 Hunter, The
139 We Merry Minstrels
141 Willie, Willie, Will
142 Young Rider
145 All Praise to Thee
150 Kyrie, Kyrie, Eleison (Lord, Have Mercy)
151 Ehre sei Gott in der Höhe
   (Glory to God in the Highest)
152 Gaudeamus (Let Us Rejoice Today)
154 Hashivenu (Turn Us to You, O God)
155 Hava Nashira (Let Us Sing a Song of Praise)
158 Masters in This Hall
159 Non Nobis Domine (Not to Us, Lord)

162 When Jesus Wept
164 Beau Printemps (Beautiful Spring)
170 Willkommen, Lieber Schöner Mai
    (We Welcome Lovely Month of May)
174 Cherubini Canon # 1
175 Cherubini Canon # 2

Medium Difficult
22 Sing with Thy Mouth
40 Fie, Nay Prithee, John
44 Jinkin the Jester
58 Antonio Salieri Scherzo Canon
66 Fester Sinn
68 Haschet (Catch the Joy)
73 When V and I Together Meet
105 Now I Walk in Beauty
120 Under the Stone
122 Ceciderunt in Profundum
    (Fallen into the Depths)
136 Two Lawyers
146 Ave Maria
147 By the Waters of Babylon
148 Cantate Domino (Sing to the Lord)
153 Geht, Hinin Alle Welt
    (Go Out Into the World)

Songs by Category

About Music and Singing
8   All Things Shall Perish
9   Auf, ihr Brüder (Get Up and Sing)
10 Come and Dance, Come and Sing
11 Es Tönen Die Lieder
    (A Shepherd Sings the Song)
12 Freunde, Lasset uns Beim Zechen
    (Friends, Forget the Cares that Bore Us)
14 Jagdgesang (Hunting Song)
15 Lachend, Lachend (Laughing, Singing)
16 Let Us Endeavor
16 Sing, Sing Together
17 Let Us Sing Together
18 Nu, Nu, Nu, Nu (Let Us Sing and Be Happy)
20 Now We Are Met
21 Oh, Music, Sweet Music
22 Sing with Thy Mouth
23 Bell Doth Toll, The
24 Viva la Musica (Long Live Music)

Animals and Critters
26 Ah, Poor Bird
27 Benji Met a Bear
28 Grasshoppers Three

156 Like As a Father
160 Sanctus (Holy)
161 Verbum Domini (The Word of the Lord)
165 Die Blumen (Flowers)
168 Sumer is Icumen In
173 Caldara Canon # 2
178 Haydn Crab Canon
180 Schubert Canon

Difficult
12 Freunde, Lasset uns Beim Zechen
    (Friends, Forget the Cares that Bore Us)
18 Nu, Nu, Nu, Nu (Let Us Sing and Be Happy)
48 O, Wollte doch der Mensch
    (Oh, If Only Man)
114 Das Licht ist Mir Erloschen
    (The Light has Faded)
126 Hark! Roars the Bellows
144 Alleluia
172 Caldara Canon # 1
173 Caldara Canon # 2
176 Crab Canon

29 Little Bird Sits in a Holly Tree
30 Marjorie
31 My Dame Has a Lame Tame Crane
32 One Duck on a Pond
33 Three Blind Mice
34 Spider to the Fly, The
35 Why Shouldn't My Goose

Friendship, Love, Peace and Conflict
38 Dona Nobis Pacem (Grant Us Peace)
39 Every White Will Have its Black
40 Fie, Nay Prithee, John
41 Go to Joan Glover
42 Here's a Health to All Them that We Love
43 Hyda, Hyda (Knowledge is Your Friend)
44 Jinkin the Jester
45 Lo Yisa Goy (He Lifted a Nation)
46 Neemt mlj in de Hand
    (Give to Me Your Hand)
47 Our Door is Always Open
48 O, Wollte doch der Mensch
    (Oh, If Only Man)

50 Pauper Sum Ego (I am So Poor)
51 Rose, Rose, Rose, Rose
52 Vine and Fig Tree
53 When I Go Home
54 Willst, du Immer Weiter Schweifen
   (Happiness is Always There)

Humorous and Clever
56 1, 3, 5, 8
57 A Ram Sam Sam
58 Antonio Salieri Scherzo Canon
60 Black Socks
61 Bubbling and Splashing
62 C Scale Canon
63 Das Hexen (The Witches Magic Square)
64 Do, Re, Mi
65 Duchess for Tea
66 Fester Sinn
68 Haschet (Catch the Joy)
70 One Bottle of Pop
72 Toembai (A Nonsense Song)
73 When V and I Together Meet

Meals and Blessings
76 For Health and Strength
77 For thy Gracious Blessing
78 Praise and Thanksgiving

Morning and Evening
80 Bona Nox (Good Night)
82 Buon Giorno Mio Caro
   (Good Morning My Dear)
83 Early As I Was Walking
84 Erwacht Ihr Schlaferin
   (Now Every Sleeper Waken)
85 Farewell Dear
86 Feierabend (Work is Finished)
87 Frère Jacques (Brother John)
88 Gone to Bed is the Setting Sun
89 Good Night to You All
90 Merrily, Merrily Greet the Morn
91 Milha Bilou Loubi Shembel
   (My Sweetest Darling)
92 Morning is Come
93 Nachtigallen Kanon (Nightingale Canon)
94 Now All the Woods Are Waking
95 Now Comes the Hour for Peaceful Rest
96 O, How Lovely is the Evening
97 Shalom Chaverim (Goodbye, Friends)
98 Sing Me Another
99 Welcome, Welcome Every Guest

Nature, Land and Sea
102 A Boat, A Boat
103 Above the Plain
104 Come Follow
105 Now I Walk in Beauty
106 I Love the Mountains
107 On the River Flows
108 Rise Up, O Flame
109 Round and Round
110 Row, Row, Row Your Boat
111 We're On the Upward Trail
112 White Coral Bells

On Death and Dying
114 Das Licht ist Mir Erloschen
   (The Light has Faded)
116 Death is a Long, Long Sleep
117 Here Lies Jack Chill
118 If You Trust
119 Old Abram Brown
120 Under the Stone

People, Places and Things
122 Ceciderunt in Profundum
   (Fallen into the Depths)
124 Chairs to Mend
125 Come to the Top of the Path
126 Hark! Roars the Bellows
128 Have You Seen the Ghost of John
129 Hey, Ho, Nobody Home
130 Little Tom Tinker
131 Derry Ding Dong Dason
131 Make New Friends
132 Martin, Lieber Herre (Martin, Dear Sir)
133 Scotland's Burning
134 Hunter, The
136 Two Lawyers
138 Little Bell at Westminster, The
138 White Sand and Gray Sand
139 We Merry Minstrels
140 Where is John
141 Willie, Willie, Will
142 Young Rider

Sacred and Latin
144 Alleluia
145 All Praise to Thee
145 Jubilate Deo (Sing Joyfully to God)
146 Ave Maria
147 By the Waters of Babylon
148 Cantate Domino (Sing to the Lord)

149 Christmas is Coming
150 Da Pacem Domine (Give Peace Lord)
150 Kyrie, Kyrie, Eleison (Lord, Have Mercy)
151 Ehre sei Gott in der Höhe!
     (Glory to God in the Highest)
152 Gaudeamus (Let Us Rejoice Today)
153 Geht, Hinin Alle Welt
     (Go Out Into the World)
154 Hashivenu (Turn Us to You, O God)
155 Hava Nashira (Let Us Sing a Song of Praise)
156 Like As a Father
158 Masters in This Hall
159 Non Nobis Domine (Not to Us, Lord)
160 Sanctus (Holy)
161 Verbum Domini (The Word of the Lord)
162 When Jesus Wept

Seasons

164 Beau Printemps (Beautiful Spring)
165 Die Blumen (Flowers)
166 Flow'rs Are Dying
167 Nicht Länger ist Winter
     (It's No Longer Winter)
168 Sumer is Icumen In
170 Willkommen, Lieber Schöner Mai
     (We Welcome Lovely Month of May)

Songs without Words

172 Caldara Canon # 1
173 Caldara Canon # 2
174 Cherubini Canon # 1
175 Cherubini Canon # 2
176 Crab Canon
178 Haydn Crab Canon
179 Minor Canon
180 Schubert Canon

Songs by Composer

Johann Sebastian Bach (1685-1750)
176 Crab Canon

Ludwig van Beethoven (1770-1827)
95   Now Comes the Hour for Peaceful Rest

William H. Bradbury (1816-1868)
92   Morning is Come

Johannes Brahms (1833-1897)
29   Little Bird Sits in a Holly Tree
141 Willie, Willie, Will

William Byrd (1540-1623)
159 Non Nobis Domine (Not to Us, Lord)

Antonio Caldara (1670-1736)
10   Come and Dance, Come and Sing
172 Caldara Canon #1
173 Caldara Canon #2

Luigi Cherubini (1760-1842)
156 Like As a Father
174 Cherubini Canon #1
175 Cherubini Canon #2

Jacobus Clemens non Papa (1510-1556)
160 Sanctus (Holy)

Ludwig Ernst Gebhardt (1787-1862)
151 Ehre sei Gott in der Höhe
     (Glory to God in the Highest)

Adam Gumpelzhaimer (1559-1625)
148 Cantate Domino (Sing to the Lord)
153 Geht, Hinin Alle Welt
     (Go, Out Into the World)
161 Verbum Domini (The Word of the Lord)

Franz Joseph Haydn (1732-1809)
48   O, Wollte doch der Mensch
     (Oh, If Only Man)
54   Willst du Immer Weiter Schweifen
     (Happiness is Always There)
63   Das Hexen (The Witches Magic Square)
64   Do, Re, Mi
66   Fester Sinn
68   Haschet (Catch the Joy)
93   Nachtigallen Kanon (Nightingale Canon)
117 Here Lies Jack Chill
178 Haydn Crab Canon

John Hilton (1599-1657)
104 Come Follow

Gustav Holst (1874-1934)
126 Hark! Roars the Bellows

Charles Frederick Lampe (1740-1780)
118 If You Trust

Roland de Lassus (1532-1594)
164 Beau Printemps (Beautiful Spring)

Wolfgang Amadeus Mozart (1756-1791)
12 Freunde, Lasset uns Beim Zechen
(Friends, Forget the Cares that Bore Us)
80 Bona Nox (Good Night)
144 Alleluia
146 Ave Maria

Michael Praetorius (1571-1621)
18 Nu, Nu, Nu, Nu (Let Us Sing and Be Happy)
24 Viva la Musica (Long Live Music)
108 Rise Up, O Flame

Henry Purcell (1638-1695)
120 Under the Stone

Thomas Ravenscroft (1582-1635)
22 Sing With Thy Mouth

Antonio Salieri (1750-1825)
58 Antonio Salieri Scherzo Canon
114 Das Licht ist Mir Erloschen
(The Light has Faded)

Franz Schubert (1757-1828)
170 Willkommen, Lieber Schöner Mai
(We Welcome Lovely Month of May)
180 Schubert Canon

Bedrich Smetana (1824-1884)
140 Where is John?

Thomas Tallis (1505-1585)
145 All Praise to Thee

Georg Philipp Telemann (1681-1767)
122 Ceciderunt in Profundum
(Fallen into the Depths)